SOMEWHERE

IN SUBURBIA

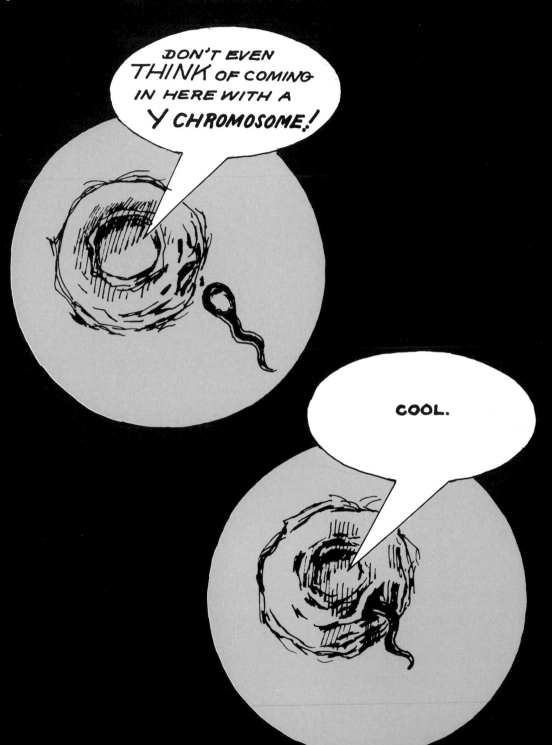

IT ALL STARTED

CHRISTMAS EVE SOMETIME IN THE 60s

WHEN HER (S)MOTHER ANNOUNCED:

SHE WAS EVEN IMPATIENT IN THE WOMB:

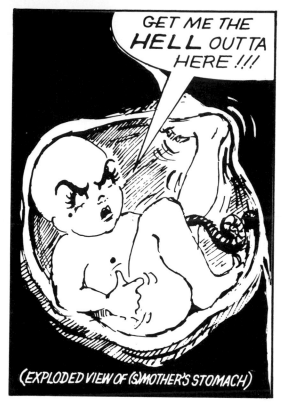

c'mon now, push

ahh...

PUSH!

ahh!!

HARDER!!!

AaAHHHH!!!!

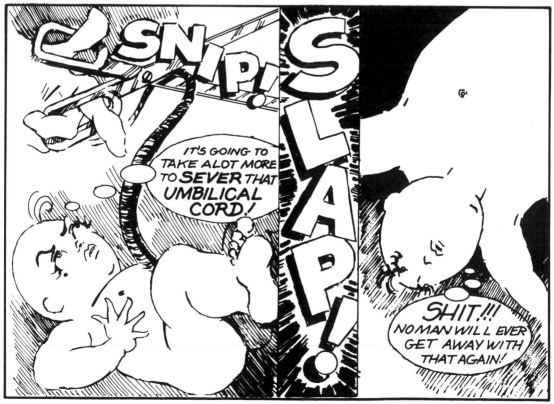

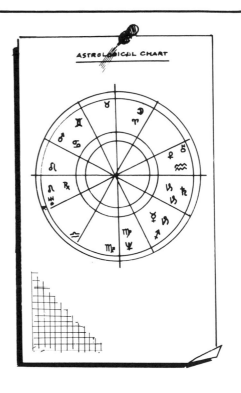

Meanwhile... a map of the stars at that very same moment:

ASTROLOGICAL CHART

SHE WAS BORN WITH THE SUN IN CAPRICORN (DUH.!), JUPITER IN THE FIFTH HOUSE (UH-HUH), SATURN IN THE SIXTH HOUSE (WHATEVER THAT MEANS), MARS IN THE ELEVENTH (WHAT'S THIS—"ASTROLOGY 101"?) AND NOW, (WHERE'S PATRIC WALKER WHEN YOU REALLY NEED HIM?) BACK TO EARTH:

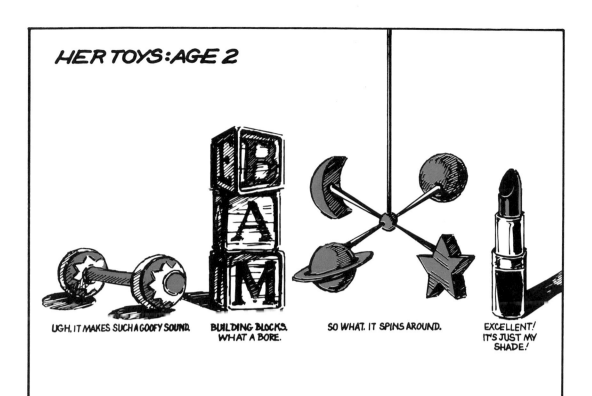

HER TOYS: AGE 2

UGH, IT MAKES SUCH A GOOFY SOUND.

BUILDING BLOCKS. WHAT A BORE.

SO WHAT. IT SPINS AROUND.

EXCELLENT! IT'S JUST MY SHADE!

We wore girdles on our bodies, and girdles on our minds.

To paraphrase Betty Friedan in The Feminine Mystique.

AND WORST OF ALL... SHE'S *BEEN SUCKING DOWN DAIRY SINCE DAY ONE:*

GREAT... IN ANOTHER *THIRTY YEARS, I'LL BE GETTING CELLULITE!*

OF COURSE, HER (WORST) FEARS WERE LATER CONFIRMED:

SHE STUDIED HER (S)MOTHER TO SEE

WHAT SHE WOULD TURN INTO.

THANK GOD FOR DONNA KARAN BLACK OPAQUE TIGHTS.

It's time for (HER FAVE--THE FAB FOUR) a musical interlude:

(TOO BAD YOU ONLY HAVE A CD PLAYER.)

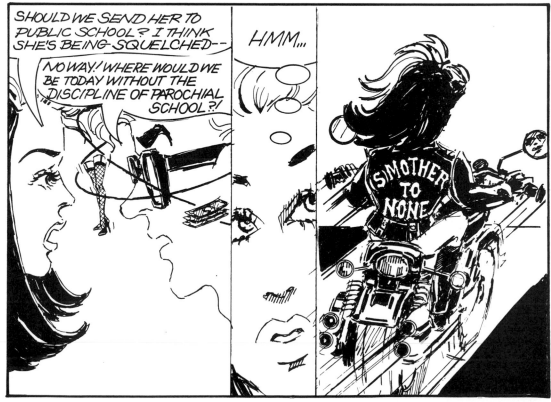

IN DEFENSE OF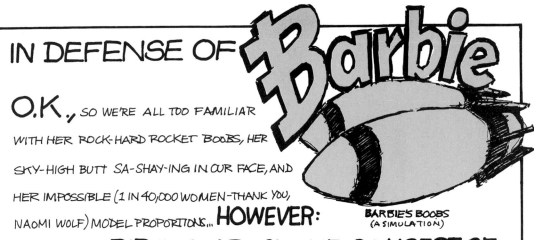

O.K., SO WE'RE ALL TOO FAMILIAR WITH HER ROCK-HARD ROCKET BOOBS, HER SKY-HIGH BUTT SA-SHAY-ING IN OUR FACE, AND HER IMPOSSIBLE (1 IN 40,000 WOMEN - THANK YOU, NAOMI WOLF) MODEL PROPORTIONS... **HOWEVER:**

BARBIE'S BOOBS
(A SIMULATION)

BARBIE DID INTRODUCE THE CONCEPT OF "MAN AS ACCESSORY" TO MIDDLE AMERICA.

YO KEN, ARE WE MISSING SOMETHING?

KEN- WITH HIS MANNEQUIN-ISH "BAD HAIR" AND HIS VACILLATING BETWEEN WUSSY (SEE ILLUSTRATION AT *LEFT*) AND BIMBO, WAS THERE FOR THE TAKING. **BUT SHE,** ON THE OTHER HAND, THOUGHT DOLLS WERE KINDA DULL......

HER TOYS: AGE 5

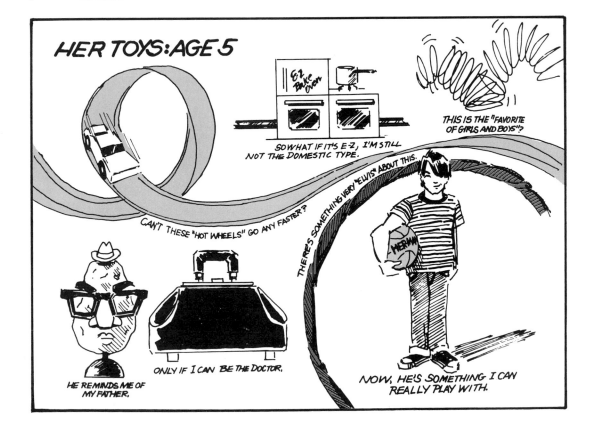

SO WHAT IF IT'S E-Z, I'M STILL NOT THE DOMESTIC TYPE.

THIS IS THE "FAVORITE OF GIRLS AND BOYS"?

CAN'T THESE "HOT WHEELS" GO ANY FASTER?

THERE'S SOMETHING VERY "ELVIS" ABOUT THIS.

HE REMINDS ME OF MY FATHER.

ONLY IF I CAN BE THE DOCTOR.

NOW, HE'S SOMETHING I CAN REALLY PLAY WITH.

SHE GOT HIT:

CRASH!

I GOT IT!!!

UGH-H-H-.!!!

PRETTY DAMN HARD.

HEY, I GOT YOU SOMETHING.

REALLY?

Note: music under: David Cassidy (sigh!) singing "I Think I Love You" from The Partridge Family's Greatest Hits.

SHE WAS BLINDSIDED BY LOVE IN A BIG WAY. AND SHE WAS OFFICIALLY "OVER" PAUL McCARTNEY. (WHICH WAS O.K., BECAUSE LATER ON WINGS WOULD SUCK.)

UMM...

WILL YOU MARRY ME?

HECK YEAH.

SHE LOVED HIM MORE THAN DAVY JONES. MORE THAN DONNY OSMOND (DUH!). MORE THAN DAVID CASSIDY.

DO YA WANNA PLAY BASEBALL?

NAH.

BASKETBALL?

YEAH.

BESIDES, SHE WAS SURE BOBBY SHERMAN COULDN'T SLAM DUNK.

PHYSICAL CONTACT RULES.

Thank you, David.

And now,
back to the 'burbs.

HEY DAD?

WELCOME TO THE CRAZY HOUSE

✶Her family put the **"fun"** in **"dysfunctional"**
before the term was even invented.

I'M LISTENING.

CAN I HAVE SOME MONEY?

THE TIM

BOY-LINDA AND I ARE GOING TO THE CORNER STORE.

FOR WHAT?

SHE WANTS TO BUY A PLAYBOY.

IS THERE A BUG IN MY SALAD?

HOW TO TELL IF YOUR DAD'S IN . . .

(do. do. do. do.) "THE"

(JUST TAKE THIS LITTLE QUIZ AND FIND OUT!)

1.Does your father know:
A.your birthday?
B.your age?
C.your name?
D.none of the above

2.You got your dad's attention when:
A.you got good grades
B.you got bad grades
C.you hit him over the head with a 2 by 4
D.none of the above

3.Your dad hid behind:
A.the paper(obviously)
B.your (Go ask your) (s)mother
C.his work
D.his car(only the non-italian & non-jew variation)

4.If your dad were a TV show he'd be:
A."The Twilight Zone" (duh!)
B."The Outer Limits"
C."Lost in Space"
D."Get Smart"

5.If your dad were a TV character he'd be:
A."The Fugitive"
B."My Favorite Martian"
C.(the back-end of) "Mr. Ed"
D.(all of)"Mr.Magoo"

6.If your dad was something you'd find in the house (fat chance) he'd be:
A.Clue?(the board game)
B.Yoo-hoo(the drink)
C.the ever elusive missing sock

7.If your dad was a song he'd be:
A."Space Oddity"(ground control to Major Tom)
B."Does Anybody Really Know What Time It Is?"
C.(the male version of) "She's Not There"

DAD ZONE"

TRUE OR FALSE:

--You consider your dad the original "Ozone Man"
--Your dad spent more time taking care of business than taking care of his family
--If he were stranded on "Gilligan's Island," your dad would have no idea he was lost
--You've seen the ghost in "The Ghost and Mrs. Muir" more than you've seen him
--He thinks the phrase "what trip is he/she on?" has something to do with vacation time
--He doesn't get it-- "what's all this fuss about 'the beetles,' [hello, "The Beatles"?] they're just annoying little bugs!"

SCORING:
(You're sunk from the start if your dad's an air[head] sign).
If you couldn't relate to anything on this test-- CONGRATULATIONS!
But if you can relate-- **JOIN THE CLUB!**

" TO DREAM... THE AMERICA, ' DREAM... "

SHE DREW FROM EXPERIENCE:

C'MON... IT'S O.K.—

UGH...

LATER:

What is a (s)mother?

OH,,,IT'S THE MOST BEAUTIFUL THING I'VE EVER SEEN!

A (s)mother helps you when you throw up.

BUT THERE WERE THOSE WHO DIDN'T APPRECIATE HER (NOT SO) HIDDEN TALENT:

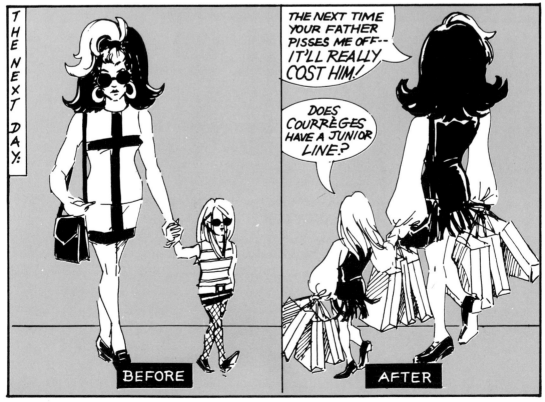

SHE AND HER-MAN WERE PLAYING "MOD SQUAD."

SHE (OF COURSE) WAS "JULIE!"

HER-MAN (OF COURSE) WAS "PETE."*

*Link, (as usual) was missing.

HEY SIN-THIA.

HEY...

...I HAVE A DANCE RECITAL TONIGHT...

...THAT I REALLY...

...WANT YOU TO COME TO...

...HER-MAN.

HEY SIN-THIA...

...WHO DO YOU THINK YOU ARE...THE HUMAN SLINKY?

OH... I DIDN'T EVEN SEE YOU!

FINE, DON'T INVITE ME. I'D RATHER WATCH (UGH!) "MY MOTHER THE CAR" ANYWAY!

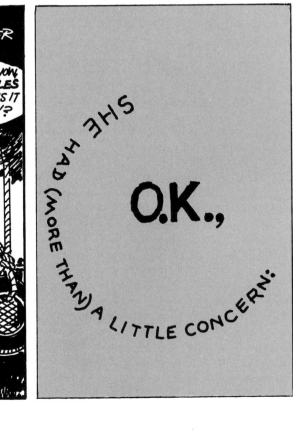

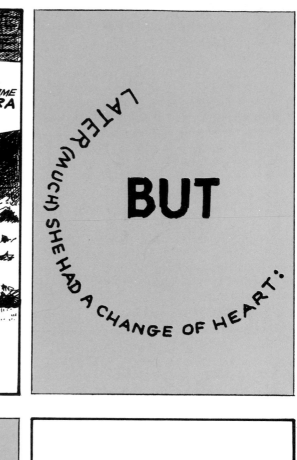

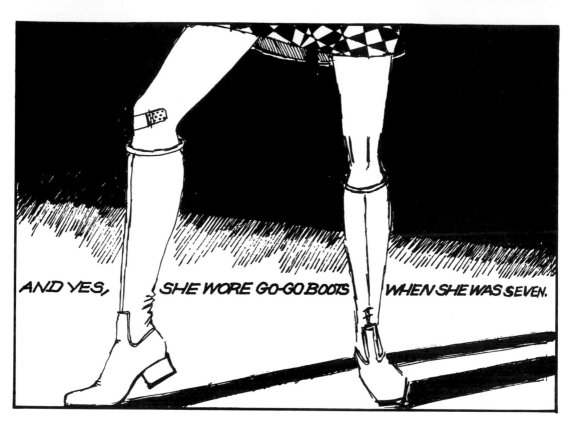

AND YES, SHE WORE GO-GO BOOTS WHEN SHE WAS SEVEN.

SHE WAS SLIGHTLY HYSTERICAL OVER (S)MOTHER'S HYSTERECTOMY:

I'LL BET ALL THE *LOVE BEADS* IN *HAIGHT-ASHBURY* SHE SHOULDN'T HAVE THIS OPERATION!

WELCOME

THE PARTRIDGE

LATER THE NEXT DAY:

OH NO!!! HER HEART STOPPED!!!

OPERATING ROOM

OH NO...

...THERE'S SOMETHING SERIOUSLY WRONG!

OUR FA THER WHO ART IN H EAVEN HALLOW ED BE THY N AME THY K INGD OM COM

OH GOD... I WASN'T EXACTLY DYING TO HAVE AN OUT-OF BODY EXPERIENCE!

OH GOD... IF YOU SAVE MY (S)MOTHER, I'LL GIVE UP STRIP POKER AND DONATE ALL MY EARNINGS TO THE CHARITY OF YOUR CHOICE. I WON'T READ THE SENSUOUS WOMAN, THE HAPPY HOOKER, OR ANY OF THE OTHER BOOKS SHE STASHED AWAY WHERE I CAN'T (OH PUH-LEEZ!) FIND THEM. AND, I WON'T SEND TELEGRAMS TO PAUL MCCARTNEY ANY-MORE. IF THE BEATLES WANT TO BREAK-UP, IT'S THEIR OWN BUSINESS!

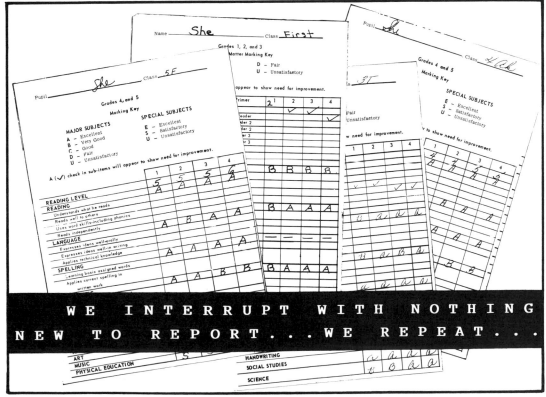

GEORGE, PAUL, RINGO, AND JOHN READ HER MIND. SHE WANTED A REVOLUTION, YA KNOW.

RUTH BADER GINSBURG, WASHINGTON, D.C.:

JUSTICES OF THE SUPREME COURT...

...ISN'T DISCRIMINATION OF WOMEN ILLEGAL UNDER THE "EQUAL PROTECTION AMENDMENT"?

BELLA ABZUG, N.Y.C.:

WE WANT IT ALL, BUT WE'LL TAKE HALF!

WOMEN MARCHING FOR EQUALITY, CHICAGO, L.A., BOSTON, N.Y., ATLANTA, MINN., S.F.:

EQUAL PAY FOR EQUAL WORK!

SHE, SUBURBIA:

Her first French lesson didn't have a lick to do with languages.

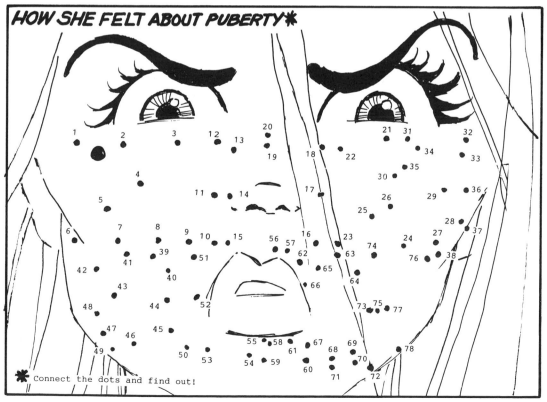

SO, thanks to her (s)mother

signs you may be (s)motherly

The "She Top Ten"* list:

10. When you were younger, your (s)mother accidentally melted Jell-O by heating it because "it's too cold for my baby!"

9. "Aurora Greenway" (Shirley Maclaine's character in Terms of Endearment) is your (s)mother's favorite role model.

8. Her favorite song: "You and Me Against the World."

7. Because you were held so tightly when you were an infant, your rib cage is slightly smaller than it should be.

6. "Shh... I think my (s)mother's on the line!"

*With apologies to David Letterman.**
**If you're a fan, turn to pages 176-177

she was more than a little mortified:

HELLO, MA?
GUESS WHAT...
SHE JUST GOT HER PERIOD!

suffocating from love:

5. She's so far in your face, she steals your oxygen.

regular rib cage   your rib cage

4. Who else would smell marijuana, liquor, or any other illegal substances on you before the thought of (ab)using them even crossed your teenage mind?

3. Her clairvoyant ability is completely uncanny: "Honey... did you lose your virginity last night?"

2. Your bags are packed. You're ready to go on a guilt trip on a moment's notice.

1. While growing up, you often wondered: "JUST WHO THE HELL IS SHE, ANYWAY?"

SHE WAS WAITING FOR HER-MAN.

NICE SHOT. DON'T YOU HAVE A DATE TONIGHT?

YUP.

SWISH! SWOSH HER-M...

BUT UNFORTUNATELY...

HEE!
HEE! HEE!
HEE!
HEE!

OH HER-MAN!

HER-MAN WAS OTHERWISE ENGAGED.

OH... SIN-THI- UGH...

OH NO.

I THINK... YOU SHOULD BE A LITTLE MORE CAREFUL...

"movin' on up (singers) movin' on up..."

Uh-huh.

She got up-graded.
To the upper rungs
  of the upper middle
    of middle class.
The split level
became a colonial.
The street became
a "cul-de-sac,"
and their driveway became
"circular."

Here it wasn't who had
  the greener grass,
but who had the
thinner thighs,
the bigger "benz"
(what year? what model?),
and the better "beemer."
(Nah! Nah! Nah!
  Nah! Nah!,
    I do! I do!)
And it was here
  that their Ford Ltd. wagon
  and their Chevy Impala
  were the only "domestics"
  parked in the "foreign" lot:

OKAY KIDS...
WE'RE HERE!!!

GREAT. IT'S OFFICIAL.
I'M LIVING
IN THE
MATERIAL
WORLD!

And yeah--
as if going to an affluent, snotty, suburban high school wasn't
nauseating enough:

WHY SHE WILL NEVER BE "MISS AMERICA":*

SHE ONLY SMILES WHEN SHE FEELS LIKE IT.

SHE DOESN'T THINK **BATHING SUIT** AND **COMPETITION** BELONG IN THE SAME SENTENCE.

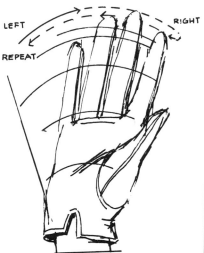

ISN'T THAT STUPID WHITE-GLOVED BEAUTY QUEEN WAVE REASON ENOUGH?

BLUE CONTACTS WEREN'T INVENTED YET.

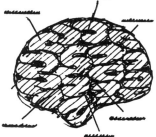

HER GREATEST ASSET ISN'T HER ASS.

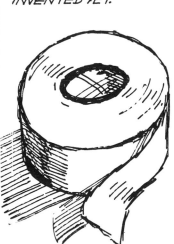

SHE WON'T MASKING TAPE HER (NONEXISTENT.) BOOBS FOR BETTER CLEAVAGE.

C'MON. WOULD YOU CONSIDER THEM ROLE MODELS?

SHE'S NOT A BLONDE. SHE'S A **DIRTY BLONDE...**

 CIRCA 1978.

O.K., I WANT TO GET THE HELL OUTTA HIGH SCHOOL. I WANT OUTTA SUBURBIA. I'M SICK OF LIVING IN THE LAND OF **LOUIS VUITTON** LUGGAGE. I WANT TO GO TO THE CITY. I WANT TO BE AN ARTIST. *BUT MOST OF ALL... I WANT OUTTA THE SEVENTIES, IT SUCKS GROWING UP IN THE DECADE OF DISCO!*

SO, LIKE I GUESS YOU WOULDN'T BE INTO **DOIN' THE HUSTLE**!

NO. BUT MAKE IT **THE CHA-CHA** AND YOU'VE GOT YOURSELF A PARTNER!

JOHN... YOUR FOURTEEN MINUTES ARE UP-- YOU HAVE ONE MINUTE LEFT!

DAMN... DOES THAT MEAN **I'LL** BE SINGING "SATISFACTION" WHEN I'M SIXTY?!

And now, Let's take a break from her past.

(TURN PAGE TO
OPEN DOOR.)

SHE HAS QUITE A FEW ROLE MODELS:

IS MY CLOSET
CENTRAL CASTING?

SHE

BARBRA STREISAND
(CIRCA 1968)
FOR THAT "DON'T RAIN ON
MY PARADE" KINDA VIBE.

EMMA PEEL
*BEFORE THEY PUT HER
IN POLYESTER.*

MARY RICHARDS
*BECAUSE "SHE'S GONNA
MAKE IT, AFTER ALL."*

MADONNA
*UNDERNEATH IT ALL
LURKS A MOGUL.*

GLORIA STEINEM
*SHE DIDN'T SKIRT
THE ISSUE OF FEMININITY
AND FEMINISM.*

NANCY SINATRA
*"THESE BOOTS ARE MADE
FOR WALKIN'," BABY.*

DIANE KEATON
WHO ELSE COULD PULL OFF
ALL THOSE (WRITER, DIRECTOR,
PHOTOGRAPHER, ACTOR) HATS?

AUDREY HEPBURN
THE EMBODIMENT
OF GLAMOUR.

OPRAH WINFREY
AT 50 MILLION AND COUNTING,
WOULDN'T YOU WANT TO BE IN HER SHOES?

HILLARY RODHAM CLINTON
*HEY--NOTHING'S MORE IMPORTANT
THAN YOUR HEALTH.*

MOTHER TERESA
*WHO COULDN'T CARE LESS
ABOUT FASHION.*

AND NOW, SORRY BACK TO THE 70s:

RECOMMENDED CUT: "BUNGLE IN THE JUNGLE".
(BUMMER, YOU DON'T HAVE AN 8-TRACK CASETTE DECK.)

SHE TOUCHED "IT." HE TOUCHED "IT."

THE "FEELING" WAS MUTUAL.

I CAN'T... I'M JUST NOT READY YET!!!

BUT HONEY, I PROMISE... I'LL STILL RESPECT YOU IN THE MORNING!!!

MEANWHILE...

SOMEWHERE IN THE SOUTH OF FRANCE:

HER DIETS: A RETROSPECTIVE

DIET PILLS
YOU THINK I'M A BITCH _NOW_...

THE ICE CREAM DIET.
GIVE ME A BIG FAT BREAK.

NO WAY. IT'S TOTALLY NAUSEATING.

THE BEVERLY HILLS DIET.
ALSO KNOWN AS "THE BEVERLY HILLS IMBALANCED DIET."

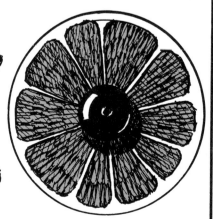

THE LIQUID DIET
NO THANKS,
I'D RATHER BE BULIMIC.

THE SCARSDALE DIET.
AFTER DOING IT,
YOU'D MURDER
THE DIET DOCTOR, TOO.

THE GRAPEFRUIT DIET.
TALK ABOUT O.D.-ING ON ACID.

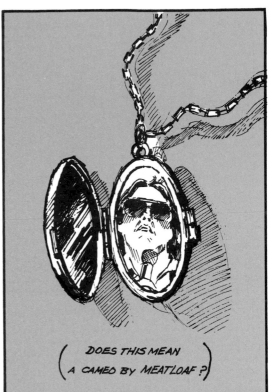

SO, SHE FLED SUBURBIA FASTER THAN
YOU COULD SAY "DE-FORMATIVE YEARS"...

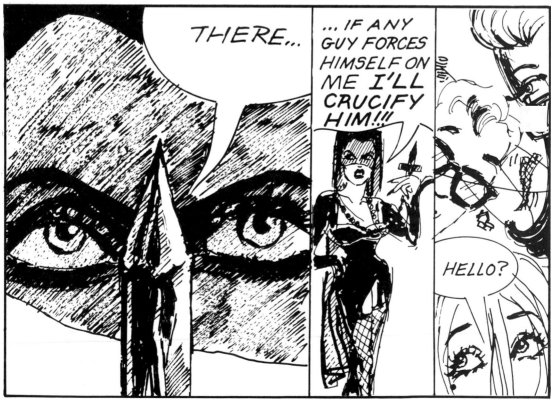

IT WAS THE MILLISECOND BEFORE

MTV ENTERED THE MAINSTREAM:

SHE WENT FROM THE LAND OF NEUTRALS TO A WORLD OF DAY-GLO.

AND I THOUGHT IT WAS A BIG DEAL TO GO BLONDER.

WHERE WOMEN PINED FOR

GUTTERGIRL AND HER LOVER

MEN WHO LOVED MEN.

GUTTERGIRL'S LOVER AND HIS LOVER

HIS NAME IS IRA, BUT WE CALL HIM BI-RA.

SUDDENLY, HER LIFE WAS LIKE A FELLINI FILM

WITHOUT THE EDITING:

BUT SEX RELEASED HER:

FASHION FREED HER:

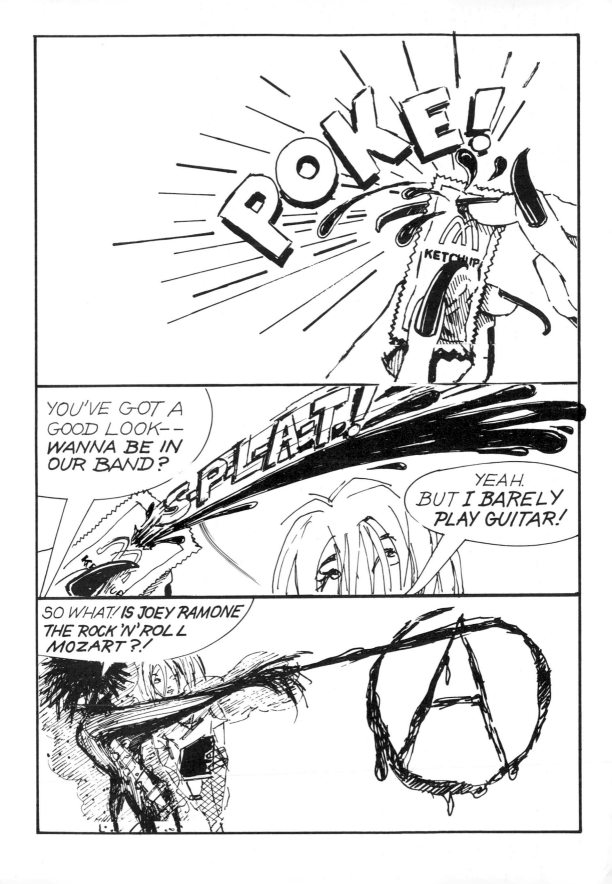

PUNK ROCKED HER:

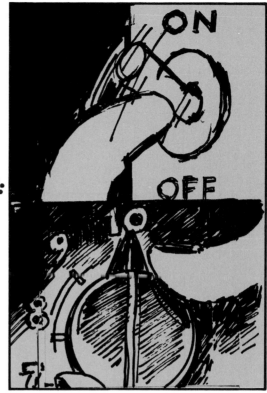

AND YET, IT WAS ART THAT DEFINED (CONFINED?) HER:

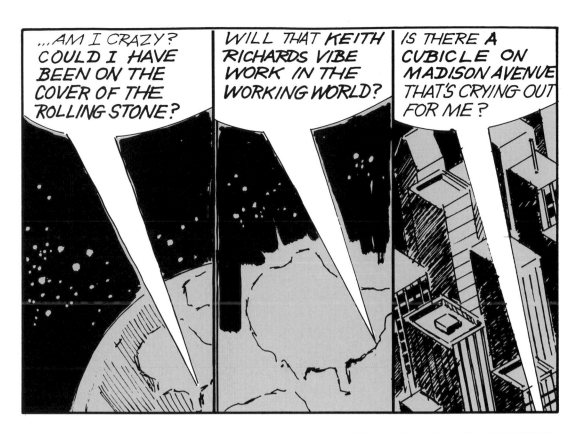

AND BEIGE, BEIGE, BEIGE*

* Not to mention gray and navy blue.

SHE WAS STRANDED IN A SEA OF SUITS

IT WAS WHEN RONALD REAGAN USHERED IN "MORNING (OR IS IT

"MOURNING*?) IN AMERICA":

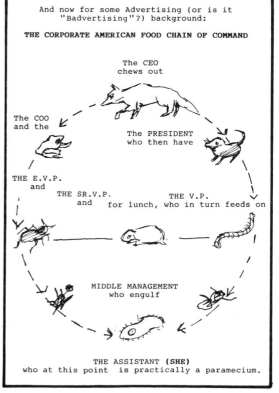

SO, THEY WENT DIRECTLY TO THEIR CORPORATE CHAIRMAN

(NO SUPERVISORS HERE--THE BREAST ACCOUNT WAS HIS PET PROJECT.)

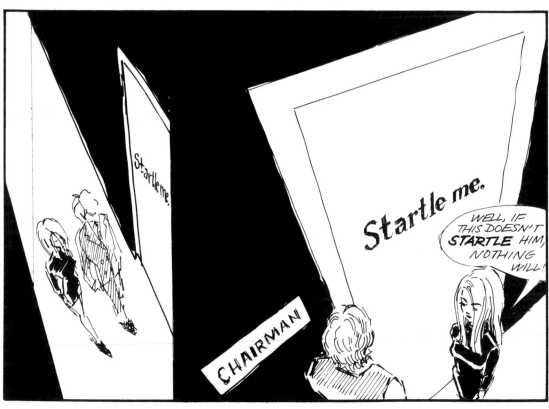

SO, WE HAVE GLYNNIS CHARLES, THE FORMER MISS USA, NOW CHICKEN MAGNATE, ADVERTISING *HER NEW BREASTS...*

AND, THAT'S EXACTLY WHAT WE DID.

WE SEE HER. TOTAL GLAM. **VERY CYBILL SHEPHERD À LA** <u>MOONLIGHTING</u>. 'CAUSE YOU KNOW SHE'S SEARCHING FOR THAT STAR VEHICLE FOR HERSELF.

WE OPEN ON A CLOSE-UP OF GLYNNIS. HER BACK IS TO THE CAMERA. **SHE SEEMS TO HAVE NOTHING ON.** SHE LOOKS OVER HER SHOULDER AND SAYS...

HI, I'M GLYNNIS CHARLES. AND I'M HERE TO SHOW YOU 250 MILLION HUNGRY AMERICANS SOMETHING YOU'VE NEVER *SEEN BEFORE...*

MY BREASTS!

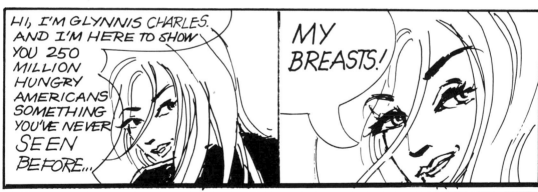

GLYNNIS, IN A **BOB MACKIE BACK-LESS GOWN** HOLDING A SILVER TRAY, TURNS TO FACE THE CAMERA AND SAYS:

MARINATED CHICKEN BREASTS EACH PREPARED IN ––

LATER, VERY LATE AT THE OFFICE:

Start me.

THERE...

HER FIRST APARTMENT* DIDN'T MEET HER LOFTY EXPECTATIONS:

*NOTE: THANKS TO SEVEN FLIGHTS UP, SHE'LL NEVER NEED A STAIRMASTER IN THE '90s.

AM I THE LITTLE OLD LADY WHO LIVES IN A SHOE BOX?!

S-T-R-I-K-E!!!

AND HER UPSTAIRS NEIGHBORS BROUGHT NEW MEANING TO THE TERM "CRASH PAD!"

WHAT THE HELL ARE THEY DOING UP THERE?!

HE ENTERED EVERYTHING ELSE
IN THE LAND OF OPPORTUNITY.

WHAT'S A GIRL TO DO? (BESIDES GET

SO...

AN AIDS TEST?)

AND *YEAH, SHE BURIED HERSELF RIGHT INTO HER WORK.*

THEN SHE HAD A REALIZATION:

BUT IT WAS WORSE (WAY, WAY WORSE):

Follow your bliss.

-Joseph Campbell

F*** this job.

                    -SHE

SHE JUST WANTED TO MAKE IT OFFICIAL: HER CAREER WAS OVER. THERE WAS NOTHING TO LIVE FOR...

SHE THOUGHT ABOUT THE CHILD SHE'D NEVER HAVE.

THE HUSBAND SHE'D NEVER MEET, WHEREVER HE IS,

OH MY GOD— I'M HAVING SEX AGAIN— THANK YOU

THE BLACK SATIN/STRETCH BRA/MINI ENSEMBLE SHE'D NEVER WEAR.

SHE COULDN'T
POSSIBLY WEAR THAT
ENSEMBLE UNTIL
SHE GOT RID OF HER
PRE-MENSTRUAL BLOAT.
(THAT WOULD TAKE
3 TO 4 DAYS, MAX)

AND *BESIDES.....*

OF COURSE, THERE WERE THOSE IN THIS WORLD(?) WHO HAD A SLIGHTLY DIFFERENT PERSPECTIVE:

YET SHE COULDN'T CONCEIVE OF HAVING KIDS WITH (ANY OF):

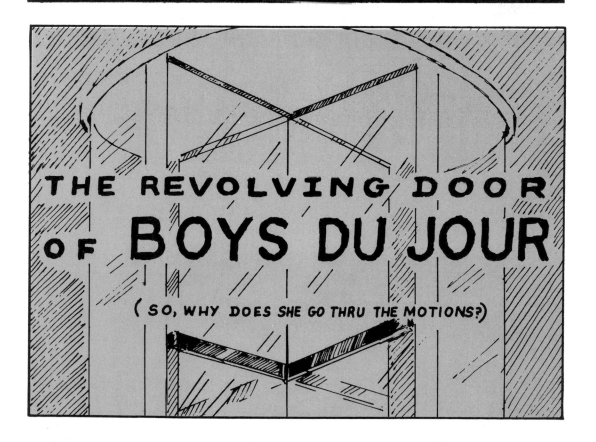

THE REVOLVING DOOR OF BOYS DU JOUR

(SO, WHY DOES SHE GO THRU THE MOTIONS?)

HER TOYS: AGE 31

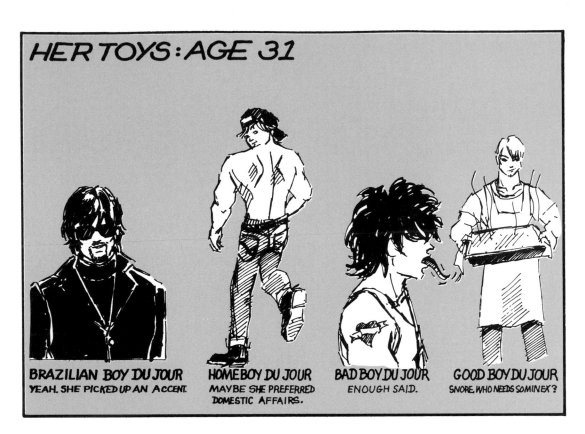

BRAZILIAN BOY DU JOUR
YEAH. SHE PICKED UP AN ACCENT.

HOME BOY DU JOUR
MAYBE SHE PREFERRED DOMESTIC AFFAIRS.

BAD BOY DU JOUR
ENOUGH SAID.

GOOD BOY DU JOUR
SNORE. WHO NEEDS SOMINEX?

ANYWAY, BACK TO SHE (WHO WASN'T JUST MADDER THAN MAD AT "MAD AVE."):

SHE WAS ANGRY WITH THE RELIGIOUS RIGHT.

HOW DOES GOD FEEL ABOUT THEM PUTTING WORDS IN HIS MOUTH, FOR CHRISSAKES?

SHE WAS ANNOYED WITH THE LEFT.

WHY CAN'T YOU SHUT UP, SINEAD?

SHE WAS UPSET WITH THE STATE OF THE UNION.

WHAT DO I HAVE TO DO TO FEEL SAFE?

SHE WAS FED UP WITH HER BOY DU JOUR.

WHAT'S WRONG?

WHAT'S RIGHT?

AND SHE WAS IRKED AT HER JOB.

DO YOU MIND WORKING AGAIN THIS WEEKEND?

DO I MIND NOT HAVING A LIFE?

BUT THERE WAS ONE THING SHE KNEW SHE'D NEVER GET OVER:

By now you must be hungry, so let's see what she has to eat.

TURN PAGE TO OPEN FRIDGE.

SO, HOW DOES SHE **REALLY** SEE HERSELF?

AND PART OF HER WANTED TO BE A NUN.

(WHICH WAS KIND OF APPROPRIATE SINCE SHE HADN'T HAD SEX IN AGES.)

extra virgin olive oil

WAS SHE ATHENA, GODDESS OF ALL WORKING WOMEN?

WISHFUL THINKING?

SHE'S ALL OF THE ABOVE.
AND NONE OF THE ABOVE.
SHE'S A MOOD RING.
A COMBINATION PLATTER.
ONE FROM COLUMN A,
TWO FROM COLUMN B.
WHICH LED HER TO...

THE ULTIMATE QUESTION:

AND JUST WHEN SHE THOUGHT IT WAS SAFE TO GO INTO HER CLOSET:

DAMN... WHO PUT THE "WAR" IN WARDROBE?

SHE WAS CAUGHT IN THE CROSSFIRE.

NAOMI WOLF BELIEVES IMAGES OF BEAUTY ARE WEAPONS AGAINST WOMEN.

HOW CAN I BE FEMININE AND STILL BE A FEMINIST?

CAMILLE PAGLIA THINKS BEAUTY IS POWER.

WHAT IF I'M HAVING A BAD HAIR DAY?

IT WAS A MIRACLE SHE EVEN GOT DRESSED IN THE MORNING.

THANK GOD FOR GLORIA STEINEM, THE PATRON SAINT OF MINISKIRTS.

SHE NOTICED THE FIRST LADY HAD TO FACE IT.

LEAVE HILLARY ALONE— SHE'S A ROLE MODEL, NOT A MODEL.

WHILE OTHERS DEALT WITH IT BARELY. MADONNA, GET YOUR TITS OUTTA MY FACE.

SHE HEARD IT IN HER PSYCHIC READING:

YOUR "BABIES IN WAITING" ARE HOVERING OVER YOU.

DAMN!... I'M NOWHERE NEAR READY FOR A COMMITMENT!

SHE HEARD IT WHEN SHE WAS EATING.

A WOMAN ONLY HAS 50,000 EGGS IN HER LIFETIME.

THANKS. I HAVE A MOUTHFUL OF CAVIAR.

SHE HEARD IT WHEN SHE WAS SHOPPING.

MOSCHINO NOW DOES CLOTHES FOR KIDS!

BUT DOLCE & GABBANA DOESN'T DO MOTHERS TO BE.

AND SHE EVEN HEARD IT WHEN SHE WAS "WITH" HER BOY DU JOUR.

WHAT COULD SHE POSSIBLY SEE IN HIM?

I DON'T KNOW--BUT I KINDA WISH THAT THAT CONDOM WOULD BREAK!

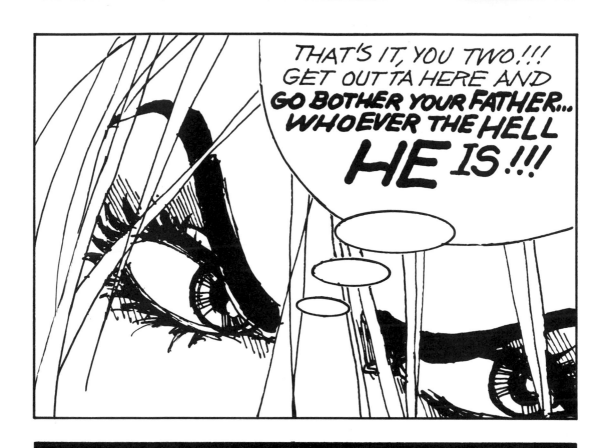

MEANWHILE, *STANDING SOMEWHERE IN THE SHADOWS OF LOVE:*

SHE WAS LOSING HER BALANCE.

THIS RELATIONSHIP IS WAY OUT OF WHACK.

IT STARTED WHEN SHE FIRST LAID EYES ON HER BOY DU JOUR.

DO YOU WANT ANYTHING ELSE?

YEAH... THAT YOUNG ONE IN THE APRON.

IN THE BEGINNING SHE DIDN'T MIND BEING SERVED,

DINNER'S READY, BABY.

HOW NICE AFTER A HARD DAY AT THE OFFICE!

The Tim

AND SHE DIDN'T MIND WEARING THE PANTS IN THE FAMILY.

WHY NOT? LONG IS IN.

BUT SHE WAS THROWN OFF-KILTER,

IS THIS BECOMING A *HOSTILE* TAKE-OVER?

EVERYTHING WAS LOP-SIDED,

CAN'T WE WATCH **CARTOONS**?

CAN'T WE WATCH **CNN** FOR CHRISSAKES?

OR ONE-SIDED.

CHECK

HIS BLADDER HAS *PERFECT* TIMING.

HER EQUILIBRIUM WENT OUT THE DOOR,

YOUR BACK IS OUT OF ALIGNMENT!

CHIROPRACTOR

MY *LIFE* IS OUT OF ALIGNMENT!

(NOT TO MENTION SHE LOST FOOTING WITH HER FRIENDS)

SO, YOU TWO *FINALLY* CAME UP FOR AIR!

I HAD TO— I COULDN'T BREATHE!

AND SHE WAS TOTALLY SICK OF BEING HIS LIFE SUPPORT SYSTEM.

SO SHE REALIZED (HELLO!)
IT WASN'T AN EQUAL PARTNERSHIP,
WHICH MADE HER WONDER:

SHE WAS LOOKING AT OTHER MEN.

HEY, THEY'RE ALWAYS CHECKING US OUT.

SHE WAS OVER THE REVOLVING DOOR OF BOYS DU JOUR.

SEE ONE. YOU'VE SEEN THEM ALL.

OF COURSE SHE'D HARDLY MIND A MAN OF POWER,

AL GORE IS LIVING PROOF THAT THE BRAIN IS THE ULTIMATE LOVE MUSCLE.

BUT NOT ONE WHO ABUSED IT.

SENATOR BOB PACKWOOD: THE "ASS" IN SEXUAL "HARASSMENT."

IT WAS AN **IMPROMPTU** MEETING OF **THE POWER BABES:**
(WHO AT THIS POINT HAVE ALL GOTTEN PROMOTED)

HELL-AYNE GOT ON THE BOARD.
ANNA-CONDA IS NOW PRESIDENT OF HER FASHION COMPANY,
LO-LISA GRADUATED FROM DOING DOUCHES TO BEER COMMERCIALS.
SANDRA (THE COMMANDA) HAS HER OWN SHOW ON MTV.
SH-HAIR-ON HIGHLIGHTED EVERY CELEB HEAD IN THE WORLD (EXCEPT HILLARY),
AND **SHE** OF COURSE MADE SR. V.P.

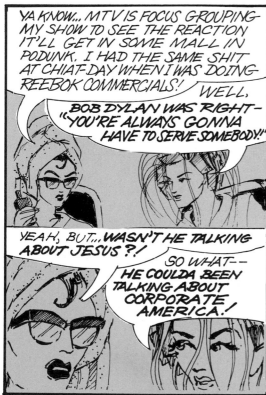

With a yell, she more...

rebel
wants

Billy Idol

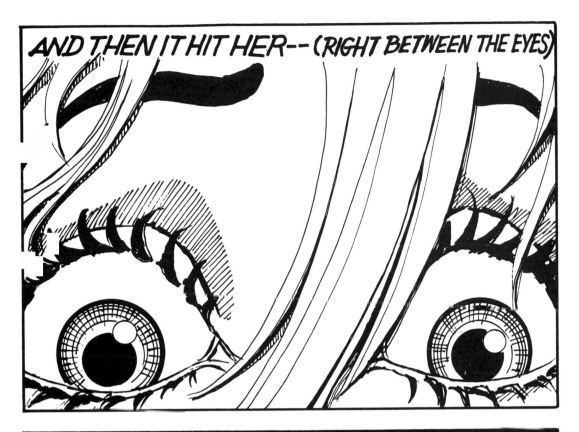

AND THEN IT HIT HER-- (RIGHT BETWEEN THE EYES)

MAYBE SHE WAS BEING A TAD SHORT-SIGHTED?
MAYBE HER VISION WAS A LITTLE BLURRY?
MAYBE CLINGING TO OLD GOALS CAUSED HER
TO HAVE A SLIGHTLY LIMITED VIEW OF HER OPTIONS?
WHY GO FROM POINT "A" TO POINT "B"
WHEN YOU CAN GO FROM POINT "A"
TO THE OPEN ROAD OF POSSIBILITIES?
WHICH BROUGHT HER TO
THE BRINK OF DISCOVERY:

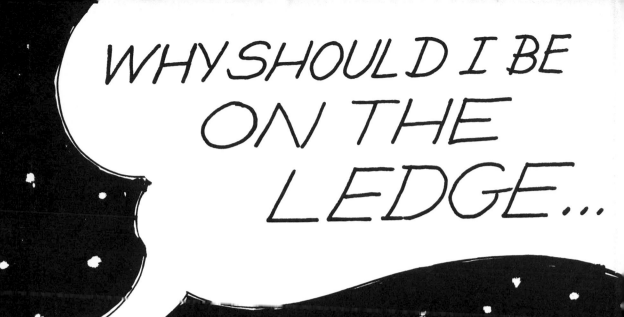

SUGGESTED MUSIC WHILE
READING THE CREDITS:
FRANK SINATRA
CIRCA 1966 SINGING
"THAT'S LIFE."

PUBLISHED BY HARMONY BOOKS, A DIVISION OF CROWN PUBLISHERS, INC., 201 EAST 50th STREET,
NEW YORK, NEW YORK 10022. MEMBER OF THE CROWN PUBLISHING GROUP.

RANDOM HOUSE, INC. NEW YORK, TORONTO, LONDON, SYDNEY, AUCKLAND

HARMONY AND COLOPHON ARE TRADEMARKS OF CROWN PUBLISHERS, INC.

MANUFACTURED IN THE UNITED STATES.

COVER DESIGN BY JOHN FONTANA & MARISA ACOCELLA

DESIGN BY MARISA ACOCELLA & JOHN FONTANA

LIBRARY OF CONGRESS CATALOGUE CARD NUMBER: 93-38695

ISBN 0-517-88294-9

10 9 8 7 6 5 4 3 2 1

FIRST EDITION

THANKS TO: BELLA ABZUG, JULIAN ALLEN, AUNT DOLLY, AUNT MARY, GAY BRYANT, MARTHA BAKER, VIVIAN BARAD, HEIDI BARON, HILARY BASS, JON & WENDY BOND, ANDY MARTIN, BILL BRADLEY, ZOE BROTMAN, ALIX BROWNE, SCOTT BURNS, THE BUSH TETRAS, AMY NEDERLANDER·CASE, OLIVIA CASE, TIM CASE, TYLER CASE, PAT BAY, LYNDA BAFF, IRA CHYNSKY, LEESA CHALK, HILLARY CLINTON, DEB JOHNSTON, D.D.A., CATHY COLLINS, NANCY COMER, SANDY CORBET, HANK CORWIN, GEORGE CLARK, TOM DECERCHIO, CARLTON DENNIS, BILLY DENAHY, CLAUDETTE DIDUL, **RAOUL DI SIBOUR— WHERE THE HELL ARE YOU?** SHARON DORRAM, LISA DULEBOHN, JOANIE EVANS, EVERYONE AT HARMONY/CROWN, EVERYONE AT MIRABELLA, JO FAGAN, DAVID FINLEY, DANA "TRIXIE" FLYNN, JOHN FONTANA, JOHN MARR, DANA GEIER, GARY GIAMBALVO, LESLIE JOHNSEN, PATTI GOLDSTEIN, AL GORE, TIPPER GORE, DR. LIZ GOREN, ALICE GREGORY, AMY GROSS, PETER GUZZARDI, SARAH HAMLIN, KELLY HAMMOND, JENNIFER HARPER, DEBBIE HARRY, HANNAH HEMPSTEAD, PAUL & TRISH HOCHMAN, HANNAH HOFFMAN, CONNIE HOFFMAN, SARAH HOLBROOK, NICK IMPALLI, HEATHER JULIUS, HEATHER KILPATRICK, SUSAN KIRSHENBAUM, LORI GREENBERG, VALERIE KUSCENKO, ROZ LICHTER, JESSICA LUSTIG, JULIA LOVRINIC, STEVE MAGNUSON, LORNA CLARKE, ANN MARINO, LAURA MARMOR, GIOVINA & RUDOLFO MAZZUCCA, HAROLD MILLER, LISA MIRCHIN, RAKESH MISHRA, AL & SHEILA MIRCHIN, STACY MORRISON, DAVE MORRISON, TERESA NICHOLAS, MARY NITTOLO, ED OTTO, ABELL OUJADDOU, LISA POMERANTZ, BRUCE PALTROW, EMMA PEEL, BETTY PRASHKER, JEFF PREISS, TAMARA RAWITT, KEITH RICHARDS, ROBERT RISKO, SUSAN ROSS, ELYSE ROTH, TIM SHERRY, MICHELLE SIDRANE, ROBERT LUPONE, BOB MORI, ELLEN SILVERSTEIN, FRANK SINATRA, MARK SITLEY, PATTI SMITH, JAMES SPINDLER, JEFF WEISS, SISSY STAMM, LAURIE STARK, DR. LINDA STONE, MICHEAL STONE, VANNA STONE, BARBRA STREISAND, CYNTHIA STUART, JULIA SZABO, ANN TABERSKI, BERNIE TELSEY, BILL TONELLI, DANNY MARINO, ELKE VILLA, THE VIRGIN MARY, DIANA VIVANTE, MARVIN WALDMAN, JIM WALSH, RICHARD WEITZ, MARY WHEELER, NAOMI WOLF, TOM WOLFE, BECKY UNDERWOOD, HUNTER MURTAUGH, DAVE ZAZULA, HY ZAZULA, HELEN ZIMMERMAN.

SPECIAL THANKS TO
BILL BORCHARD, HELAYNE SPIVAK, RICHARD KIRSHENBAUM, DAVID GREENBLATT, BINKY URBAN

SHAYE AREHEART
MY EDITOR/SISTER WHO MEANS THE WORLD TO ME. THANK YOU. YOU'RE "ALL HEART!"

AND

GRACE MIRABELLA
THE PATRON SAINT OF SHE

FOR MY FAMILY: DINA, DAVID & ANTHONY

DEDICATED TO
MY (S) MOTHER (WHO EXPECTED IT)
AND MY FATHER, WHO'S OFFICIALLY
OUT OF "THE DAD ZONE"